W9-BBX-556

To Ann, on whom I declare
my dependence —R. W.

For Arrow —W. H.

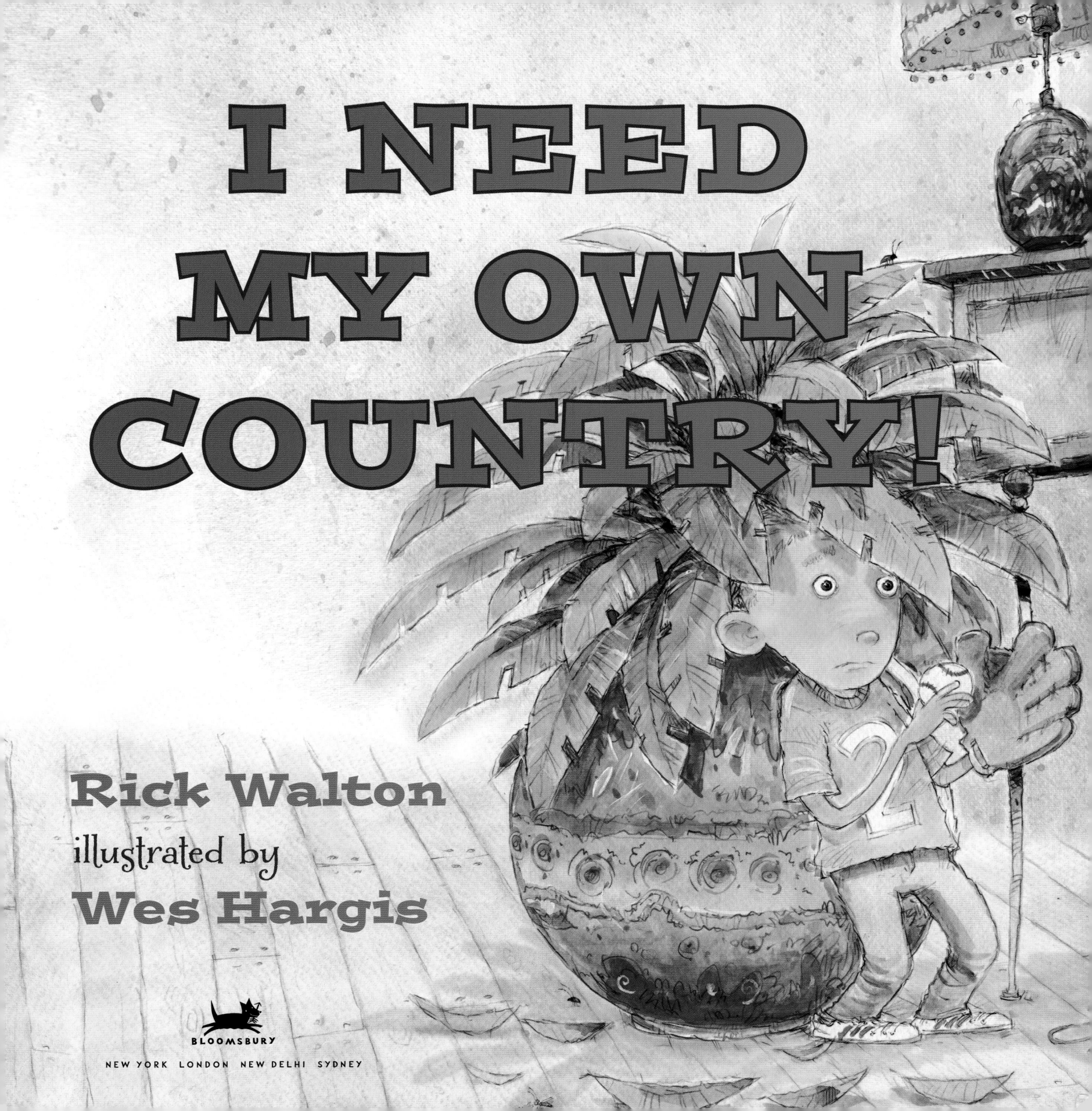

I NEED MY OWN COUNTRY!

Rick Walton

illustrated by

Wes Hargis

BLOOMSBURY

NEW YORK LONDON NEW DELHI SYDNEY

There comes a time in all kids' lives when they need to create their own country.

When this happens to you . . .

The first thing you will do is
decide your country's location.

You will need a name
for your country

and a flag.

You will need citizens.

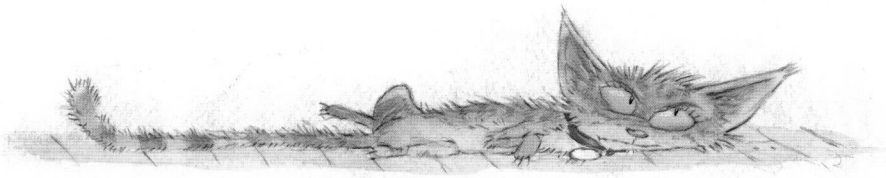

You will need to make rules.

And punishments for
breaking the rules.

You will need to choose a leader.

And that leader will need help.

You will want a national anthem,

national money,

a national bird,

and other
national things.

Not all will go well.

There will be
civil unrest.

And natural disasters.

And there might
be invasions.

You will want to
defend yourself.

When the battle is over, there will be speeches and singing.

And life in your country will get back to normal.

Foreign leaders will visit your country.

And you will visit their lands.

You may have to eat their food.

Sometimes foreign visits
don't go as planned.

So you'll prepare
for another invasion.

But be careful. They may be coming in peace.

You will accept their peace offering, because friends are more fun than enemies.

Bird
Menu
Menu
Menu
FISH
Kitty
GUEST
BUGS
MR. DRAGON
Menu
Menu

You might even
change your rules.

Which you can do—

because, after all,

it's your country.

Text copyright © 2012 by Rick Walton
Illustrations copyright © 2012 by Wes Hargis
All rights reserved. No part of this book may be reproduced or transmitted in any form or by any means, electronic or mechanical, including photocopying, recording, or by any information storage and retrieval system, without permission in writing from the publisher.

First published in the United States of America in October 2012
by Bloomsbury Books for Young Readers
www.bloomsburykids.com

For information about permission to reproduce selections from this book, write to
Permissions, Bloomsbury BFYR, 175 Fifth Avenue, New York, New York 10010

Library of Congress Cataloging-in-Publication Data
Walton, Rick.
I need my own country! / by Rick Walton ; illustrated by Wes Hargis. — 1st U.S. ed.
p. cm.
Summary: Instructs the reader in how to form one's own country when the time comes, from finding a location, a name, and a flag, to handling the inevitable civil unrest and invasions.
ISBN 978-1-59990-559-4 (hardcover) · ISBN 978-1-59990-560-0 (reinforced)
[1. Family life—Fiction. 2. Humorous stories.] I. Hargis, Wes, ill. II. Title.
PZ7.W1774Ilah 2012 [E]—dc23 2012004902

Typeset in Liam
Book design by Nicole Gastonguay

Printed in China by Hung Hing Printing (China) Co., Ltd., Shenzhen, Guangdong
(hardcover) 10 9 8 7 6 5 4 3
(reinforced) 10 9 8 7 6 5 4 3 2 1

All papers used by Bloomsbury Publishing, Inc., are natural, recyclable products made from wood grown in well-managed forests. The manufacturing processes conform to the environmental regulations of the country of origin.